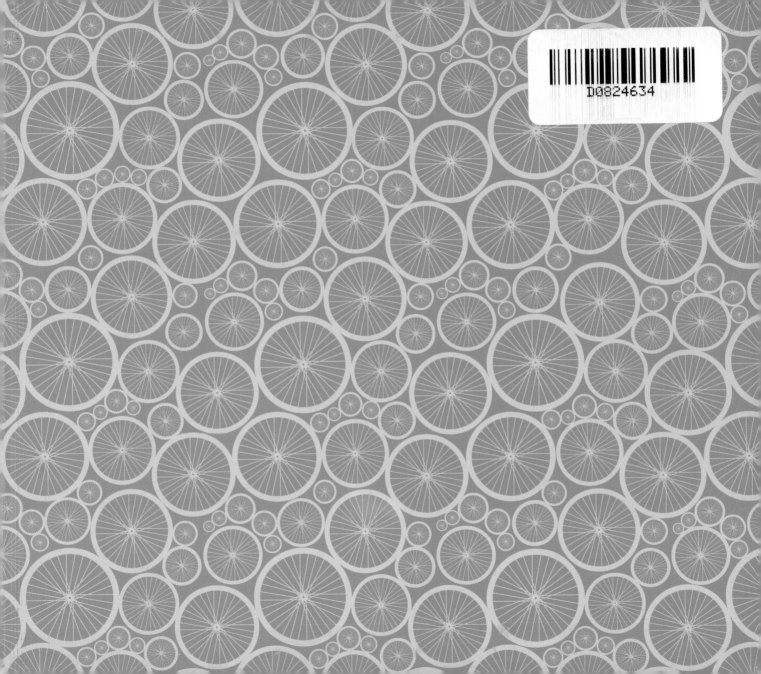
D0824634

GOGGLES
&DUST

THE HORTON COLLECTION

GOGGLES & DUST

Images from Cycling's Glory Days

VELO press

Boulder, Colorado

Copyright © 2014 by Shelly and Brett Horton

All rights reserved. Printed in Korea.

No part of this book may be reproduced, stored in a retrieval system, or transmitted, in any form or by any means, electronic or photocopy or otherwise, without the prior written permission of the publisher except in the case of brief quotations within critical articles and reviews.

velopress®

3002 Sterling Circle, Suite 100 • Boulder, Colorado 80301-2338 USA
(303) 440-0601 • Fax (303) 444-6788 • E-mail velopress@competitorgroup.com

Distributed in the United States and Canada by Ingram Publisher Services

A Cataloging-in-Publication record for this book is available from the Library of Congress.
ISBN 978-1-937715-29-8

For information on purchasing VeloPress books,
please call (800) 811-4210, ext. 2138, or visit www.velopress.com.

This paper meets the requirements of ANSI/NISO Z39.48-1992 (Permanence of Paper).

Photo retouching by Elizabeth Riley
Design by Vicki Hopewell

14   15   16 / 10   9   8   7   6   5   4   3   2   1

■ ■ ■

On the cover:

Jef Demuysere and Gaston Rebry, 1929 Tour de France
Wheel to wheel on the Col Bayard, stage 14

FIRST EDITION

This first edition includes a limited run of 200 hardbound copies in custom slipcases, numbered and signed by the authors, and 26 hardbound copies in custom slipcases, lettered A to Z, signed by the authors, each containing an original pre–World War II racing photograph.

The authors gratefully acknowledge the cooperation of the Bibliothèque nationale de France, the moral rights holder of many of the photographs in this book.

For Trevor

INTRODUCTION

From the turn of the 20th century through the late 1930s, cycling was an important part of a magical era. Bicycle racing, particularly stage racing over Europe's snow-covered peaks and along its unmade roads, quickly became the continent's most popular sport, creating an ambience that was both grueling and romantic. While the names of the great riders were celebrated with increasing fervor in the daily press, the races devised to showcase their abilities became diabolically difficult. To draw crowds and sell newspapers, race directors sought the most difficult routes, the highest passes, the hardest conditions, the longest distances. The 1926 Tour de France, for example, spanned 5,745 kilometers,

or 3,570 miles, over a mere 17 stages. Today's much more humane and realistic races, by contrast, run about 3,400 kilometers over 21 stages.

The giants of the sport endured all this and more, and their names have been carved into cycling immortality. Many are represented here, including André Leducq, Georges Speicher, René Vietto, Nicolas Frantz, Learco Guerra, Ottavio Bottecchia, Maurice Garin, Antonin Magne, Roger Lapébie, Eugène Christophe, Lucien Buysse, Honoré Barthélémy, and Maurice De Waele. The events these riders contested made them the leading sports heroes of their time, and their feats and legacy have been celebrated in cycling literature ever since.

Yet while written accounts of the races have been told and retold over the years, the photographs from this period have become increasingly scarce. As commercial photo libraries have become consolidated over the decades, and as the conversion to digital archiving has enforced a de facto selectivity, the variety and number of images available for general viewing have shrunk.

This consolidation of available photographs has had a pernicious effect on our appreciation of the sport because the contemporary images of the events and people capture the soul of bicycle racing in a way that is nearly impossible with words alone. It is only when one studies the etched lines on the faces of the riders as they toil up a rutted, muddy mountain road that one appreciates the true difficulty of the era's contests. And as we linger over the images, we then notice the joy in the eyes of the fans, both young and old, who stand along those same roads to cheer and encourage their heroes.

The story further unfolds when we see the slumped shoulders of the defeated rider, the joyous upthrust arms of the victor coming across the finish line, the concerned mother watching the peloton that includes her son race by the doorstep of the family home. All provide gripping glimpses of the impact of the sport on the lives of the competitors and their fans during a time that witnessed incredible advances across nearly every facet of life while it devastated the land with two catastrophic wars.

Emerging from the ashes of World War I, cycling did its part to unite communities and countries, providing a sense of hope and normalcy on the heels of a very challenging time in history. Races across Europe, particularly the Tour de France, embraced riders from many countries. The races gave reasons to celebrate life. Despite the difficult conditions, communities would come together to prepare their village for the passing of the peloton. While resources were meager, a town's citizens would break out their finest clothes, often well-worn and carefully mended, to celebrate the arrival of a race. The effects of war and the economic depression that followed are clear to see, both in the racers' clothing and equipment and in the conditions of the places they visited.

. . .

As much as we treasure the photographic evidence of these times, I must admit that my wife, Shelly, and I never set out to collect original vintage bicycle racing prints. In fact, the only reason we initially acquired them was to document and help authenticate some of the older racing jerseys and accessories in our collection.

However, life has a way of leading one in strange and often wonderful directions. Through nothing more than dumb luck, over the course of several years we were able to assemble an ever-increasing number of original photographs and negatives that focus exclusively on racing from the late 1800s through the 1970s. We found photos at auction, through other collectors, and at flea markets while also acquiring the photo archives of a few defunct periodicals. It wasn't until recently that we began to inventory the photos and realized we had amassed more than 350,000 original images!

Today, for us, it is an absolutely transcendent experience to sit down with a folder containing a stack of images of a specific rider from many years ago. In these photos, careers are captured and brought to life. In some cases we may have five or six photos of a rider, whereas for others we have collected several thousand. It is in those comprehensive folders that you see the fresh-faced amateur who turns pro, rides to many triumphs, and then ages before your eyes. For many of cycling's champions, the end of their racing did not mean an end to their relationship with the bike. Many went on to be part of race organizations, to run teams of their own, or to open bicycle shops in their hometowns.

The longer Shelly and I have had the opportunity to enjoy these photos in our care, the more special they have become and the more we have come to realize what an honor it is to have stewardship of them. To introduce our son, Trevor, to these images and to watch his interest grow has made the collection even more rewarding.

For this book, we focused narrowly on the first four decades of the last century, striving always to find dramatic images that not only were representative of the races of their time but also have not been widely reproduced. In fact, most of these images have not been printed since they first appeared in the newspapers and periodicals of the day. We tried to select the best available representation of each image. In some cases, we have both the original negative and multiple enlargements to sort through. In other cases, a lone and sometimes damaged print is the sole artifact available.

Which brings up the somewhat thorny issue of originality. Although each of these photos comes from an original negative or a print made from that negative, all of the images printed in this book have undergone some degree of restoration. Water stains, fingerprints, and the occasional splash of cognac have been removed. Scratches, smudges, crop marks, dust specks, clumsy previous attempts at retouching, smears and streaks have been carefully excised and banished. None of this work has been applied to the original negatives and prints, which remain in as-acquired condition. But for this book, we felt it best to restore the photos as nearly as possible to new condition so that the beauty and wonder of them could be clearly presented to a fresh generation of fans.

We hope you enjoy them as much as we do, and we look forward to sharing many more images down the road.

—*Brett Horton*

5

René Vietto, François Neuville, Raoul Lesueur, Henri Puppo, Jean Fontenay

■ ■ ■

Col de la Gineste team time trial

Vietto leads his Helyett-Hutchinson team

Gino Bartali

■ ■ ■

1938 Tour de France

Bartali won both the overall and the mountains classification

André Leducq

∙ ∙ ∙

1928 Tour de France
Refreshment after the Perpignan–Marseille stage finish, stage 11

René Vietto

∎ ∎ ∎

1935 Tour de France
Taking supplies before a day in the saddle

René Le Grèves

■ ■ ■

1937 Tour de France
Replacing his chain, which had unshipped on the cobbles

Lucien Buysse

■ ■ ■

1926 Tour de France
Celebrating overall victory in Paris

Learco Guerra and Alfredo Binda

■ ■ ■

1930 Tour de France
Climbing the Col d'Aubisque, stage 9

Ottavio Bottecchia

■ ■ ■

1927 portrait

This photograph was taken in the year of the champion's untimely death

René Vietto

■ ■ ■

1934 Tour de France
In triumph after stage 11 victory in Cannes

14

Gaston Rebry

∎ ∎ ∎

1929 Tour de France
Between Vannes and Les Sables d'Olonne, stage 6

René Vietto

■ ■ ■

1934 Tour de France
At the top of the Col d'Allos

Maurice De Waele, Giuseppe Pancera, Jef Demuysere

▪ ▪ ▪

1929 Tour de France
Awards ceremony, Parc des Princes

Raymond Decorte

▪ ▪ ▪

1928 Tour de France
At the stage 3 finish in Dinan

Nicolas Frantz, André Leducq, Ernest Neuhard

▪ ▪ ▪

1928 Tour de France

Stage 6 winner Frantz with teammates and awards committee

André Leducq

∎ ∎ ∎

1930 Tour de France
Leducq nearly abandoned after this crash but rejoined and won in Paris

Roger Lapébie

∎ ∎ ∎

1937 Tour de France
The Tour winner with his wife and daughter

Peloton

■ ■ ■

1938 Tour de France

The race crawls through the mountains on a "hot, terrible day"

Raymond Decorte, Julien Vervaecke, Odile Van Hevel

■ ■ ■

1928 Tour de France
Stage 12 from Marseille to Nice

Gaston Degy

∎ ∎ ∎

1923 Tour de France
Fatigue and frustration

24

Lucien Petit-Breton

■ ■ ■

1913 Tour de France
Crash on the way to Valenciennes, stage 14

Bernard Van Rysselberghe

. . .

1930 Tour de France
At the finish in the Parc des Princes

26

André Leducq

■ ■ ■

1934 Critérium des As

Victory pose

Antonin Magne

■ ■ ■

1934 Grand Prix des Nations

Attacking the time trial just after the start

Georges Ronsse and Charles Meunier

■ ■ ■

1929 Paris–Roubaix

In the feed zone: Meunier won the race; Ronsse finished second

Georges Speicher

■ ■ ■

1935 French national championships
The victor is surrounded by police and fans

Gaston Rebry

■ ■ ■

1929 Tour de France
Stage 15, Grenoble to Evian

René Vietto

∎ ∎ ∎

1935 Tour de France
Pre-race, stage 7

Eugène Christophe

■ ■ ■

1925 Tour de France
Christophe's final Tour, age 40; he finished 18th

33

Ottavio Bottecchia

∙ ∙ ∙

1925 Tour de France

With his fans after a long day in the mountains following stage 13

Paul Egli and Maurice Archambaud

∎ ∎ ∎

1936 Tour de France

Stage 1 finish in Lille in a downpour; Egli won the stage

René Vietto

• • •

1938 Tour de France
Climbing the Col du Galibier, stage 15

Various riders

∎ ∎ ∎

Race unknown, circa 1920
Midrace water break

Robert "Toto" Grassin

• • •

1925 six-day race, Paris
Post-race bath

Charles Pélissier

■ ■ ■

Portrait

Signed by Pélissier to his friend, René Vietto

Learco Guerra

∎ ∎ ∎

1933 Tour de France
Summit of the Aubisque

Roger Lapébie and Maurice Archambaud

* * *

1933 Tour de France

Lapébie assists Archambaud on the Col d'Allos

Victor Fontan

■ ■ ■

1928 Tour de France

Joined by his wife after stage victory

42

Roger Lapébie

∎ ∎ ∎

1937 Tour de France
Summit of the Col d'Allos, stage 9

Charles Pélissier

■ ■ ■

1931 Tour de France
Receiving the stage winner's kiss, Les Sables d'Olonne, stage 5

André Leducq and Nicolas Frantz

■ ■ ■

1928 Tour de France

On the road to Marseille, stage 11

André Leducq

∎ ∎ ∎

1927 Tour de France
The stage winner taking a victory lap in the Parc des Princes

Learco Guerra

∎ ∎ ∎

1936 Giro d'Italia

Italy's great champion on stage 9 from Firenze to Cesenatico

Eugène Christophe

◼ ◼ ◼

Circa 1912

Christophe won three consecutive stages in the 1912 Tour de France

Nicolas Frantz

■ ■ ■

1927 Tour de France

Stage 5 team time trial, Cherbourg–Dinan

49

Antonin Magne and André Leducq
. . .
Tour de France, circa 1928
Fixing the inevitable punctures

Lucien Buysse

■ ■ ■

1926 Tour de France
Descending the Tourmalet, stage 10

Frans Bonduel and Lucien Buysse

■ ■ ■

1930 Tour de France

Bonduel won stage 17 and finished seventh overall; Buysse did not finish his final Tour

Lucien Buysse

■ ■ ■

1926 Tour de France

Stage 3, Metz–Dunkerque: Buysse took the race lead on stage 10 and held it to Paris

René Vietto and Edward Vissers

■ ■ ■

1939 Tour de France

Summit of the Tourmalet, stage 9: Vissers won the stage; Vietto retained the race lead

54

Lucien Buysse

■ ■ ■

1929 Tour de France
Stage 18, Strasbourg–Metz

Lucien Buysse

■ ■ ■

Paris–Roubaix, year unknown
Leading the peloton into Beauvais

Picnic

∎ ∎ ∎

Tour de France, circa 1930
Fans awaiting the arrival of the race

Henri Cornet

■ ■ ■

Portrait

The 19-year-old winner of the 1904 Tour de France posing with his supporters

Maurice De Waele

. . .

1927 Tour de France
One of the 1927 Tour's five mountain stages

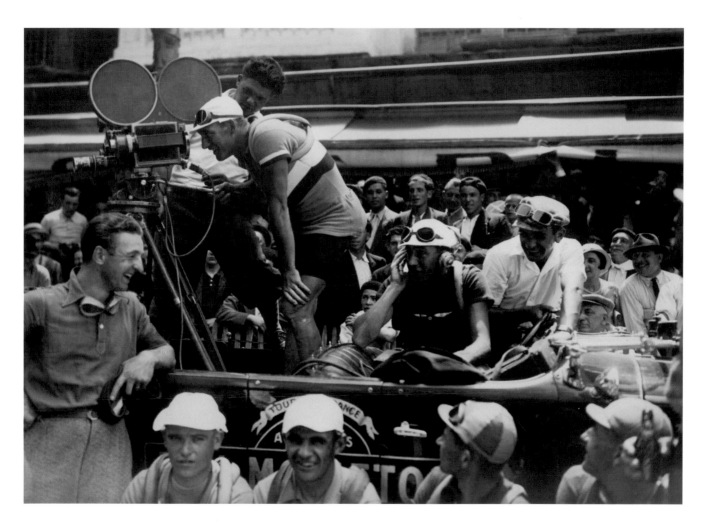

André Leducq and Georges Speicher

■ ■ ■

1933 Tour de France
Skylarking at the stage 15 start in Perpignan

Ottavio Bottecchia

• • •

1924 Tour de France

The race leader between Nice and Briançon, stage 10

Charles Pélissier

∎ ∎ ∎

1931 Tour de France

Spinning out the kilometers between Brest and Vannes, stage 4

Rider unknown

∎ ∎ ∎

1931 Tour de France

On a hot day, a rider stops for water between Marseille and Cannes

Nicolas Frantz and Maurice De Waele

■ ■ ■

1927 Tour de France
Stage 23, Charleville–Dunkerque; Frantz and De Waele finished one-two overall

64

René Vietto

■ ■ ■

1935 Tour de France
Postvictory, Aix les Bains, stage 6

Maurice De Waele and Vicente Trueba

1928 Vuelta al País Vasco
Stage 1; De Waele prevailed in the four-stage event

Nicolas Frantz

◼ ◼ ◼

1924 Luxembourg national road race
Frantz won 12 consecutive Luxembourg road championships, 1923–1934

Rider unknown

■ ■ ■

Tour de France, circa 1926

A midrace break, an adoring fan

68

Lucien Buysse

• • •

1925 Tour de France
Headed home on stage 18, Dunkerque–Paris

7.7.34. 5e étape B....... Ercam du Tour de France cycliste. A. Magne détenteur du maillot jaune est accaparé par les collectionneurs d'autographes avant son départ de Belfort.

Antonin Magne

■ ■ ■

1934 Tour de France

Signing autographs in the yellow jersey, Belfort, stage 5

H. 8. 34. le vainqueur du Tour de France a. magne va continuer a rouler
le voici dans la cour de sa ferme au volant de la luxuente voiture qu'il

3622-RJi

vient de s'offrir — "Magne" la luxuente qu'il que lui a offert un de ses
admirateur n'a aucun egard pour la carrosserie comme le montre cette
photo.

Antonin Magne

■ ■ ■

1934 Tour de France

Posing for a joke photo in his new auto after winning the Tour

Honoré Barthélémy

∎ ∎ ∎

1921 Tour de France
Climbing the Galibier, stage 11

72

Nicolas Frantz

. . .

1928 Tour de France
Climbing the Col d'Allos, stage 13

Oscar Egg

■ ■ ■

Portrait
Publicity photo circa 1919 of the great Swiss three-time hour record holder

74

Various riders
▪ ▪ ▪

Tour de France, circa 1925
Midrace refreshment

Léon Despontin

■ ■ ■

1925 Tour de France

Despontin, winner of the touriste-routier class, poses after stage 2

Victor Fontan (leading) and Maurice De Waele

■ ■ ■

1929 Tour de France
Climbing the Col du Tourmalet

Maurice De Waele

■ ■ ■

1927 Tour de France

De Waele's truss bicycle frame on display

Buffalo 10·9·33. 9ᵉ Prix Nations. Le coureur Montero est blessé à la suite d'une chute

Luciano Montero Hernandez

■ ■ ■

1933 Grand Prix des Nations
Being led through the infield after a crash, Buffalo Velodrome, Paris

Buffalo 8-9-35 Grand Prix des Nations - Magne effectue le visage crispé par l'effort, le dernier tour qui lui donne la victoire

Antonin Magne

· · ·

1935 Grand Prix des Nations

Magne won three consecutive editions, 1934–1936

10.7.34 Tour de France - Étape Aix les bains - Grenoble
L'Espagnol Ezquerra en plein effort dans le Galibier, au sommet
duquel il est arrivé 1er

Federico Ezquerra

■ ■ ■

1934 Tour de France
Climbing the Galibier, stage 7

Maurice Garin

∎ ∎ ∎

1903 Tour de France

With the Tour's first trophy; track star Edmond Jacquelin at left

Various riders

■ ■ ■

Rouen–La Bouille–Rouen, 1911

Race restricted to entrants weighing 100 kilograms (220 pounds) or more

Frans Bonduel

■ ■ ■

1932 Tour de France
Bike repair after a hard crash, stage 14

Antonio Pesenti

∎ ∎ ∎

1931 Tour de France
Summit of the Col du Galibier

Maurice Archambaud and Jean Aerts

• • •

1933 Tour de France

Catching up on the news before the stage départ, Belfort

Maurice De Waele

■ ■ ■

1929 Tour de France
Midrace repair

Maurice De Waele

■ ■ ■

1929 Tour de France

Double visors, double goggles, one spare tire, and a musette

Maurice Archambaud

∎ ∎ ∎

1935 Tour de France

Exhausted after winning a 63-kilometer individual time trial, stage 14B

Nicolas Frantz

∙ ∙ ∙

Tour de France, circa 1928
Stage end in the rain

Maurice Archambaud

■ ■ ■

1935 Tour de France

Signing autographs prior to the race start, stage 1

Maurice De Waele

• • •

1926 Circuit de Vosges–Alsace
Climbing the Ballon d'Alsace

Montmorency 22-1-39: Cross cyclo-pédestre Prix Pasteur. Un passage difficile de l'épreuve

remportée par Oubron

92

The chase

■ ■ ■

1939, Montmorency, France
Ideal conditions for cyclocross

Henri Pélissier

■ ■ ■

1923 Tour de France

Pélissier won the race by 30 minutes over Ottavio Bottecchia

Maurice De Waele

■ ■ ■

1927 Tour de France
Refreshment at the "Fontaine de Serdinya"

16.4.33 course cycliste Paris-Roubaix

Rider unknown

■ ■ ■

1933 Paris–Roubaix
Lunch on the fly

Maurice Archambaud, André Leducq, Georges Speicher, Roger Lapébie

. . .

1935 Tour de France

Post-race, stage 5

Honoré Barthélémy

∎ ∎ ∎

1921 Paris–Brest–Paris

His glass eye protected by goggles, Barthélémy refreshes on the road

René Vietto

■ ■ ■

1939 Tour de France
Attacking on the Col de Vars, stage 15

Victor Fontan

■ ■ ■

1928 Tour de France
Pre-race massage

Honoré Barthélémy

∎ ∎ ∎

1921 Tour de France

Barthélémy won two stages and finished third overall

Benoît Faure

■ ■ ■

1930 Tour de France
Attacking on the Col d'Aubisque

Jean Rossius

■ ■ ■

1914 Tour de France
Stage 10 between Nice and Grenoble

Leon Scieur

■ ■ ■

1920, race unknown

Scieur won Liège–Bastogne–Liège in 1920 and the Tour de France in 1921

Giuseppe Olmo

∎ ∎ ∎

1932 Milano–Torino
Buying a sweet before the race

Various riders

■ ■ ■

Tour de France, circa 1930
Teams sit for a meal while spectators fill the windows

Le gardeuse d'oie

∎ ∎ ∎

1939 Tour de France

The peloton passes on stage 10 from Toulouse to Narbonne

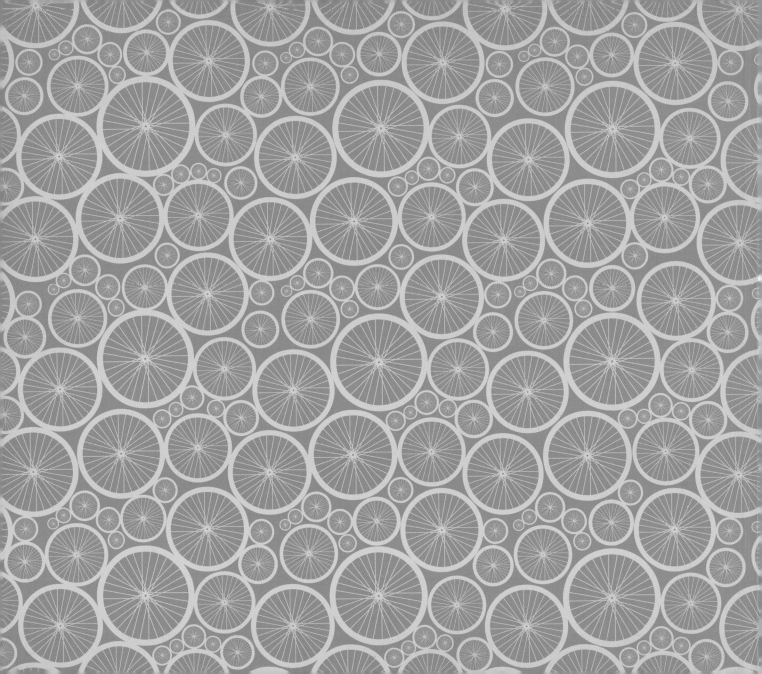